INNER REFLECTIONS

Poems by Nailah Abdus-Salaam

authorHOUSE®

AuthorHouse™
1663 Liberty Drive, Suite 200
Bloomington, IN 47403
www.authorhouse.com
Phone: 1-800-839-8640

First published by AuthorHouse 4/9/2009

ISBN: 978-1-4389-5869-9 (sc)

Printed in the United States of America
Bloomington, Indiana

This book is printed on acid-free paper.

CONTENTS

Part Three
Loves Stories

Part Four
The Precious Earth

Part Five
Ties That Bond

Part Six
Reflections

In the name of Allah Most Gracious Most Merciful

All praise is for Allah
We praise him and seek his help and forgiveness
And we seek refuge in Allah, The Most High
from the evils of our selves and from the evils
of our actions. Whomsoever Allah guides, none
can misguide him. And whomsoever Allah has
misguided none can guide him.
I bear witness that there is no god worthy of
Being worshipped except Allah alone,
without partner or associate. I further bear
Witness that Muhammad peace and blessings be upon him
is his servant and Messenger. May Allah The Exalted
bestow his peace and blessings on the Final Prophet
Muhammad(SAS) upon his good family, upon all his
noble companions, and all of the rightly guided predecessors.

ACKNOWLEDGEMENTS

A key element in the success process is nurturing relationships with those who believe in you and your goals.

To my beloved family and friends who encouraged me to gather and complete this project and fulfill my goal of publishing

This book of poetry and bring this dream into fruition.

To my mom, Rosalyn Russell and my sister Gail Suggs who listened to countless editing of a work in progress, and who remained patient, honest and encouraging.

To my dear friends whose stories and dreams inspired me to continue until this book was complete.

To all the people whose stories and personal experiences that were shared, I hope I have given justice and shown empathy and compassion in telling your story. To all of you, with the deepest gratitude, I dedicate this collection of Poetry: "Inner Reflections"

PART ONE

A Muslim Woman

I am a Muslim Woman

Simple yet complexity
all of these qualities
are in me.
I am humble
I am shy
I seek the truth
Til the day I die
I am modest
I am honest
I have dignity
I am trustworthy
I am intelligent
I am unique
I have morals
I am sweet
I am soft spoken
I keep my word
I am a good friend
I am a Muslim Woman

ONE UMMAH
ONE BODY

We're all one Ummah
We all know there's no deity worthy of worship other than Allah's
We all worship our Lord
We worship him alone
We all make salat
We pay our zakat
We fast the month of Ramadan
We make Hajj, We make Umrah
Some of us make Hijrah
We all want Jannah Al-Firdous.

We all hear the same talks
We all get sound advice
Being amongst the Muslims
Is always beneficial and nice
We eat the same foods
We all cry the same tears
We have the same fears
That our deeds are magnified
Fore death is near.
We are all sisters to one another
And brothers to each other
Who love for Allahs sake
We are all alike
In this is no mistake

One Ummah

But, yet there is animosity
Dwelling in our community
Why can't we love for each other
What we love for ourselves
Especially when it involves polygyny.
There is intolerance, impatience

And haste to backbite
Why can't we love our sisters?
By doing what's just and right
We all have the same basic needs
No matter what part of the world we call home
Remember we are 6 million standing strong
We must respect individual differences and love those
Things we have in common
We must practice the Sunnah
And be compassionate with one another.
We'll greet one another warmly
No matter where we come from.
We must make our Ummah strong for ourselves
And for generations to come.

We must become one.

One Ummah
One Body

THE TRUE AND REAL BEAUTY

What do you see when you look at me?
Do you see someone oppressed or someone free?
Muslim women are free and not oppressed.
This is the way we choose to dress
not showing our beauty for the world to see,
This right is reserved for our husband,
Our children, and family.

When you see me covered and fully veiled
don't perceive it as a weakness,
nor being timid nor frail.
Don't think we're oppressed,
because we choose to be fully dressed.
My body isn't for all eyes to see
We protect our honor and modesty.
This Hijab is a mark of piety.

Muslim women are respected
and live life with dignity
not exploited by the media or by the T.V.
In this society, to be shy is looked at with disdain,
but pleasing the people is an objective
you will never obtain.
While displaying your beauty
you think is a womanly thing.
These qualities you think will attract more men
but, Muslim women are modest and unique,
a praiseworthy characteristic for all to seek.
Some of you say, "I couldn't be you," but if you
knew the blessings and the reward
you would rush to cover up
and not be an object of lust and bad morals.

When you walk down the street

half naked and bare,
revealing your adornments for the world to share
where's your shame, your honor, and dignity
How can you be respected, when everything we see.
If you feel no shame you will do as you will
clothed but naked, and you think this has appeal!

True beauty lies in the essence of modesty.
It is also the ultimate femininity.
Her veil she wears for no eyes to see
It's not oppression --- It's liberty!!
Freedom from the men at prey
lust and immorality are all at play.

So don't think we are oppressed
because we choose to be fully dressed.
Covered women are a hidden treasure
reflect on this to realize none can measure,
to the True and Real Beauty of the Muslim woman.

WE ARE ONE

I am a Woman like you are
I am a Muslim like you are
I am a mother like you are
I am a daughter like you too
I am a wife just like you
You and I are not so different after all
Our intrinsic goals are the same
We may be from different places
And go by different names
You may speak another language
But our communication remains
There is much that binds us together
You are my sister
Now and forever
I want for you
What I want for myself
We are one
If nothing else.

A Priceless Possession
"Time"

Tomorrows not promised
There's no guarantees
You could be here today
And gone tomorrow.
Would you trade a life of play and amusement
For an eternity of sorrow?

Will you be pleading in the end,
To have one more try.
To change your life to obedience
Before it's your turn to die.

Do you take for granted
That you will wake to another day,
While wasting time, doing nonsensical
Things, amusement and play?
There are two blessings
Which many people lose
Health and free time
We must not abuse.

We cannot return the days that past
But, we can use our time wisely
By making each day better than the last.
There is no strength nor power
But with Allah ,
Who is well able to extend or shorten
Our life span.
While each breath brings us closer
To death; glad tidings you want at hand.

Truly we belong to Allah
And to Allah we shall return.

So make preparations
To return to your Lord
With excellence of character
And deeds of high score.

Let this be a reminder to me and to you.
Our departure draws near,
So strive for good deeds and be of good cheer.
Take heed that preparation is made
For the questions to be asked in the grave.

In the book of Allah it says,"give glad tidings   to those who believe
And work righteousness that their portions
Is gardens, beneath which rivers flow."

Now I ask you; Is the entertainment
of this world worth more than the joy
Of tomorrow?
Gardens of bliss where you will feel no pain,
No troubles, no sickness ,
No wild desires to tame.
Good news for this day!
If we live in this world as a stranger,
For the dunya is cursed,
And everything pertaining.

The best companions are those
Who are best in character
Have you taken the time
To say a kind word or help a friend in need?
As you well know,
A friendly smile, and acts of kindness
Are all counted as good deeds.

Again we should remember
That this life is full of shortcomings,

But showing love to your sisters
Can be a benefit to others.

Take advantage of the time
That you now receive
Before it's too late
Before we all leave
This world is but a quick passing enjoyment
With many pleasures and much adornment.
Time is
A priceless possession
If we use it well
Treasure it
Guard carefully how it is used
Remember the blessings of Jannah
And you won't waste time nor abuse it.
This priceless possession
Time

INNOVATING

Innovation
Is an ocean
With no boundaries
It can swallow you up
And drown you
In a vast looming sea
It can destroy you
With falsehood
And contrary iniquity

Don't be swayed
By the flowing tides
That can drift you far away
    Any Innovation
Will ultimately lead you astray
With lies and falseness
You will never have success

Actions not from the Sunnah
Or the book of Allah (Ta'ala)
Will always be rejected
 All acts of biddah
Must invariably be corrected
Innovating takes you far amiss
Unfortunate borders
Leading to abyss.

DO IT NOW SISTER

After my babies are grown
I'm going back to school
And finish my degree
Make life better for my children and me
I'm going to make Hajj
A trip I've been waiting to take
A journey of a life time
For Allah's (subhanna wa ta'ala) sake
After my babies are grown
I'm going to take better care of me
Long hot soaks in the tub
Cascading bubbles
With my favorite oils and rubs
I'm going to exercise more
Eat healthy and stay in shape
I'm going to spend time relaxing
Outdoors by the lake
Sipping on my herbal teas in my favorite glass
I might even take some creative Art class
After my children are grown
I'm going to start a business of my own
Become an entrepreneur
Learn Arabic, travel to Egypt and Morocco
But, until my children are grown
This life of mine is not my own
Still, there's this little voice inside of me
That's whispering constantly
Why are you waiting?
Do it now sister
And you will see
You could be growing
And accomplishing your dreams
You've got the time and you've got the means
While educating and nurturing
Your children too

You could also be doing some things for you
Do it now sister
Before the children are grown
And you find yourself living all alone.

SELF-INVENTORY

Are you watching
The way you behave
Are you seeking knowledge
From the cradle to the grave?

Are you calling yourself
To account today
Before Allah calls you
To account tomorrow
When no kind acts will go unnoticed
And no good deeds can you borrow

When your limbs
Will testify
As to what you did
On that day
It's all about how you lived

So guard your tongue
Restrain your eyes
Protect your ears
And limit your smile
Lower you gaze
Before your gaze is lowered
For on the day of reckoning
There will be total exposure

Say your prayers
Before prayers are said over you
In the grave
There will be nothing you can do.

Judge yourself today

Before you are judged tomorrow
And increase in good deeds
So you won't experience this sorrow.

Control your desires
Or your desires will control you
Shaitan is cunning
And he can be patient too.

Are you forgetting
That on Judgement Day
We will be told to stand
Barefoot, uncircumcised
Not beholding
To any man.

Evaluate yourself
Before you are evaluated
By Allah
Death is coming
It's coming for us all
We all have an appointed time
May this prose serve to remind.

PEACE

To seek a house
And acquire a home;
To seek employment
And discover enjoyment.
To secure good friends
Who will be there through thick and thin.
To seek the truth
And learn about Islam.
To seek religion
And become a Muslim.
To prepare for the worst
But expect the best.
To have faith
No worries, no distress.
To be blessed with a union unique
In its simplicity
A righteous spouse endowed with
Love and mercy.
To find myself
Alas achieving these things.
To gain happiness and peace
This is all I need!

TRUTH AND LOVE

The things we do
Will soon be past
Unless we do the things that last.
Acts of charity and good deeds
Passing on knowledge to our future seeds.
The life we build
Will never stand
If we build it on sinking sand.
The worldly things
For which we slave
Can never bring us from the grave.
Our most cherished things
May come and go
Goals and dreams may change
But truth and love
Will forever be the same.

THE IDEAL MARRIAGE

I am in a loving, passionate marriage
Our foundation is strong
Structured by the guidelines of Islam
Applying the Sunnah
And obeying the Quran
We are rooted in abundance
And generosity
Intellectual equals
With compassion and chemistry
My husband is my companion,
Lover, and good friend
We enjoy spending quality time
Each day and until the day ends
We openly express our gratitude
For this bestowed blessing.
We honor each others privacy
And sometimes a need for space
We don't make this an issue
This is all part of Allahs grace
Even in a moment of anger
He never raises his voice
In matters of the heart
My dear,you always have a choice
We have endured our challenges
With a thankful heart
Kindness and patience
Is the key
If you believe in
Not til death shall we part.
For the life of this world is short
And its treasures are few
A righteous spouse
Is a mercy
If we knew this to be true
An Ideal marriage

May never be obtained
But, it's always worth the effort
If happiness is what you gain.

Supposed To Be

Marriage
used to be held
in such honor
A blessed union
where two people gathered
with intentions
to spend their life together
A joyful union
rooted in love and mercy
But
Something drastic has changed
when now a days
many marriages end in disdain

It once was a life long commitment
Now we're acting like it's a fad
When once they were grateful
And patient
Through the good times
And the bad
Longevity
was the ultimate goal
and staying together
many blessings unfolded
But
Now days
Marriages end so fast
We enter upon it
not expecting it to last
People will see you on the street
Ask," how's married life?"
You answer," it's sweet"
The next time they see you
You're singing that ole song
First he was here

Now he's gone
We have trivialized an important decision
Without sticking it out
Nor trying to mend it
Marriage is supposed to be for a life time
But the tables have turned
Drastically, when now it's over
Before you're barely in it.

Gossip

It
travels
swiftly as a train
maligning
and destroying
causing
grief and pain
wounding
and maiming
defying
and defaming
It
topples countries
and dismantles industries
It wrecks havoc
and cuts like a knife
It destroys marriages
It can ruin your life
It generates grief
penetrates like a thief
It causes jealousy
creates envy
perpetuates misery
It becomes
a rapidly moving entity
ruining reputations
severing ties
polluting friendships
with slander and lies
It breeds
Suspicion
and the evil eye

When it comes whispering around
Just let it pass you by

Don't listen
with an attentive ear
Just say,   Halt!
I don't wish to hear.
If you can't speak good
Say nothing at all
And don't repeat gossip
That you're told
Silence is Gold

PART TWO

Say Brothers

THE SILENT CRY OF THE MUSLIMAH

Oh brothers
Hear our cries
Our voices weary
Tears now dry
The heart of the community
Is fractured
Shattered
Marriage
Then divorce
Is becoming
A dangerous habit

Open your hearts
Open your minds
Stop wasting the sisters
Energy and time
Open your eyes
Look around you
And see
How many of you brothers
Have had at least three?

Three women in the same community
All sharing the burden
Of reckless immaturity
When at the first sign of discord
You're ready to flee
Your only resolve is
To pronounce divorce
No restitution
No remorse
In another three weeks
On to the next course
    Next,
Muslimah

You're going through
Faster than
The purchase of brand new shoes
We're not your girlfriend
We are your wife
Aren't we supposed
To be together for life?

We're not like any other
Women you knew
We're pious and righteous
And beautiful too
Then why are we
Mistreated and abused
First you want us
And there's nothing you won't do
Once you have us
Then you're through
Your only resolve
Is I'm divorcing you
Impromptu divorce
Over a temporary crisis
That would soon pass
If you would just be patient while the difficulty last
Oh brothers
Hear our cry
The heart
Of the community
Is going to die.
Just love us for Allah's sake
The Muslim ummah is at stake.

JUST LIKE ME

You've gone and got another wife
Someone who equally adores you
Someone who is planning
      on building a life

                Just like me

Hanging on to your words
    like they were gold
Not realizing her time
     is growing old
Thinking that she understands
         your soul

                Just like me

You're going to break another heart
     You're going to leave her too
She'll never know what made you go
       Or why she's feeling blue

                Just like me

She will always wonder
    What went wrong
Cause she thought your love
       Was strong
She'll cry a spell
Thinking time will tell
She'll try to hold on
But as swiftly as you came
     You're gone
It may take her a while
Before she comes to realize

             She's Just like me.

Did You Think of Her

Homeless
Shaken, no where to go
Put out of the house, with kids in tow
Did you wonder
Where they would sleep
Or when she could get her clothes
Or what she would eat
Did you think of her
Knowing she was the only Muslim
From her family's house
And now she's not welcome
To even sleep on the couch
Did you wonder
What she would do
And how was she to get the kids to school
I'm not talking about a stranger in your life
She was the one you chose to be your wife
And now she's left to fend alone
The loss of you has wrenched her soul
For you were the part which made her whole
The sudden shock
The hard impact
Did you take the time to think
You may want her back
Did you know you broke her heart
With your coldness and lack of thought
A door you closed
So another door opens
For another man
To come in unfolding
And mend her shattered heart
And think of her
As his beloved wife
This time for the rest of her life.

A GREAT MAN

A great man shows
His greatness
By the way he treats the little man

A great man shows
Compassion
By acts of kindness and quickness
To lend a helping hand

A great man shows
His greatness
By the way he treats his wife

A great man
Shows his greatness
Everyday on his journey of life

By upholding the truth
And correcting the wrong

A great man shows his greatness
By being a leader
A great man is strong

The Prophets were the best
Examples of what leaders
Should be
They excelled the utmost
In all of these qualities.

The best of men were the Prophets
Who came to guide mankind
They were all great men

But these days
A Great man is hard to find.

THE WRITING ON THE WALL

Smiles have changed to sternness
no more kisses at the door
stolen moments are obsolete
last night you slept on the floor
no more sweet caresses
no glances of undressing
no more moments of laughter shared
nor spontaneous kisses to show you care
smiles have changed to indifference
tension steady on the rise
no more gifts
no surprises
silence is running golden
truth be told
I'm knowing
The writing is on the wall
The beginning of the end
is looming
in this fragile household.

DOWN TO THE BONE COOL

Black men
radiate a coolness
that's unsurpassed
They exhibit control
Even under duress
Unparalled confidence
when it comes to cool
Black men
effortlessly set the rule
An innate quality
that can't be reproduced
It can't be copied
nor manufactured to you

It's in their style
and the glide in their walk
It's in their masculinity
and the confident way
they talk
Fluent and smooth
A relaxed poise they exude
and undisputed sway
Black men have a swagger
that calls to persuade

A coolness
A passion
Embraced with humility
reveals a positive aura
and an alluring quality
It can't be learned
It can't be duplicated
You can't fake it
Nor can it be imitated
It can't be cloned

It's a deep profound coolness
Down to the bone
When it comes to coolness
Black men set the tone.

COLORS OF THE EARTH

People come in all colors
Like the Earth
Red, white, brown, and black hues
A wide spectrum of colors
All unique and beautiful
Some are black as a black stone
On a pitch black night
Black as midnight in the Congo
Striking
And so full of light
Chocolate, mocha
Mahogany bright
Sweet and rich like the Earth at night
Some are natural browns
From olive to caramel
Copper to sandalwood
Tropic sunkissed and lustrous as well
Bronzed brown skin
Happy faces with a glowing grin
Like the gold of Africa
Or the Middle East
Where the yellow cub reclines
In golden wheat grasses
That flourishes
And grows tall the fastest
West Indies brown
Sahara gold
Mellow, yellow
Full of soul
Radiant as the sun
Like a Jamaican tan
Exotic and tropical
Light as the sand
In a desert land
Or Indian red

Russets like falling leaves
Like a red breast robin
Hiding amongst the trees
Pearly white
Clear as ivory
Beige sensations
With simmers of cream
White as the Nile
In Jordans sea
Colors of the Earth
Red, black, brown, and white
A visual tapestry
People of all colors
Living in harmony.

Slow Down

You're always in a hurry
Baby
I think it's time you slow down
Sometimes you move so fast
Your feet barely touch the ground

You're always in a hurry
Baby
Rushing headlong in haste
But can you have the grace
To slow down your pace

So we can dance in unison
Beneath the stars
Under moonlit skies
Or enjoy a nice slow walk
Along the beach
Or through the park
Let's talk in the midst
Of twilight
Under the gazebo
Let's drop out of sight

If you would just slow down
We could dance through the night
Slow down
Baby
You're moving too fast
If you would just slow down
We could make this moment last.

THE GRASS ISN'T ALWAYS GREENER ON THE OTHER SIDE

Like a thief to the night
Slowly he crept into my heart.
But, not to love and cherish it forever,
Only so he could break it apart.
"I love so deeply, and it is true
That I do love you," he said.
When did Love become an excuse to flee,
His footsteps where they led.
Sometimes the grass looks greener on the other side
But, one day you will come to realize
That what you needed you had all the time.
It was through my experiences that I knew,
That love is unconditional , you must have
Patience and faith through the good and bad times too.
But, instead of patience you chose haste
Now you're remorseful, what a waste.
You didn't know at the time, you gave up something good
You didn't work to save it, by giving it the best you could.
When people don't communicate and express what it is they feel,
Subtle hurts will grow and expand
Leading to frustration and even despair.
Solutions and guidance are always available
By calling on our Lord.
Just asking for help and patience,
could have made a difference between marriage and divorce.
So now our divorce is final, and your new marriage begins
Did you think it would be peaches and cream,
When looking to new pastures,
It's not like what it seems.
When the honeymoon is over, this is when reality begins.
The grass looked so appealing
Until the day to day trials and tribulations set in
Now you have so many questions,
Why did I choose to explore?

When what I really wanted
Was waiting at home behind the front door
I already had a good woman
In all aspects of the word
Virtuous and beautiful
Who obeyed me and feared her Lord.
In a short span of time;
This new marriage comes to an end,
But now I've lost my first wife,
Lover, and my friend.
The future cannot correct the moments
And time loss
Now, I see by thinking the grass is greener
I paid an exorbitant and very high cost.

WHAT'S THE LESSON

What's the lesson
When so many words are associated
With the color black
As something negative
Derogatory and a personal attack
Black is Beautiful
Black is the color of my people
Who are strong and live with dignity
But if you look up Black in the dictionary
This is what you will see
They say Black is
Soiled
Dirty
And
Angry
Wicked
Dismal
And
Gloomy
Absence of light
Lacking knowledge and foresight
Evil
Dismal
Black as a moonless night
 Black market
Blackmail
Black death
Where a plague prevails
Black widow
Which is like a venomous snake
Who will bite off his head and kill her mate
Black heads
That clog the skin
Black balled
To be voted out again

Black guard
And
Black list
Black out
Come out at your own risk
Black sheep is the one
Who is a disgrace to his family
Why are all these connotations
Disparaging to me
Not only to me
But to our entire race
These attributes are a terrible disgrace
This does not describe our nature
Or basic qualities
These words aren't specific
To you nor me
Each of us defines who we are
These words promote lack of self-worth
Self hatred and can leave open scars
It goes to show though much has changed
Some things remain the same
What's the lesson
When you don't even know your name?

LIES

When I look you in your eyes
    the cold disguise
Of questionable and wise
      Decisions
    I say no lies

Spoken words spinning
    out of control
no substance no truth
  But you're on a roll
  Your speech is fast
A race car driver
  plunging down the path
    I say no more lies

  Your voice is raised
    Words cascade
    Unconvincing myriad
    Half-truths and lies
Can be seen in your eyes
I'm deafened to the sound
Coming from your voice
    Cause baby,
  You've got a choice
      No more Lies

PERPETRATE

My prospective
Intendee
During our courtship
Be honest with me
                    Shoot it to me straight
Don't bombard my mind
Confuse my thoughts
Just to
Facilitate
Your desires
To consume me
With intangible intention
You rush in
Not to contribute
But to take

Issues are hidden
And obscured
Character is false
A recipe for disaster
Divorce is the final cost
        In Islam
We're given ease
No need for falsehood
No need to deceive
                    If you don't perpetrate

Through me
A dwelling place
Of tranquility
A peaceful repose
For those who believe

Shoot it to me straight

Be forth coming
Wit your status quo
Honest communication is best
For that's what I need to know
And be upfront with my dowery
Something of worth
That shows you value me

Do disclose
And don't conceal
Secrets in time
Will all be revealed
Can you live
In kindness
And respect
A nurturing love
But never neglect
There are many issues to discuss
For you are in charge
Of a mighty trust
And if you don't

       Perpetrate

Through my wakil
We can have another date.
Another meeting
For us to see
If this is where I'm supposed to be
A righteous man
Is what I need
Who values me
And implements his deen.

AUTHENTIC FREEDOM

Richness is not in having
many belongings
but real richness
is the richness of the soul.
Acquiring wealth and fame
should not be our goal
Where is the peace
in more is best
Contentment comes
to those who have less
True success comes from within
success isn't measured
by external things
obtaining objects can't make you free
they demand more companions
more possessions to see
Racing to pursue superficial entities
will leave you enslaved,
not happy nor free.
Look to those who have less
as a measure of success
Freedom cannot be purchased or won
but,
By simplifying you life
Authentic freedom will come.

From A Dream to a Nightmare

Your eyes once gleamed and sparkled
Your smile lit up the room
But now, when you cross the threshold of home
Your face is filled with gloom.

I see your mood is not the same,
Words unspoken, and your demeanor
Has drastically changed.
this is so unfamiliar,
You have stepped far out of range.

You roam the streets at night
Not returning home until daylight.
Wandering with no foresight,
To the affect and harm done to others
Your wife, your son, and even your mother.

I don't know where you are
Or where you have been
Yet you say suspicion is a sin.
The secrets you hold on to,
I fight to break the silence
To get through to you.

Your struggles have become mine too.
Sleepless nights, loss of appetite
The secrets, the lies,
The excuses, the alibis.
What is real? What is real!
When you can't believe your eyes.

Truth has changed to lies.
The mask you wear, your disguise.
I don't see the man I knew
So does that mean our love wasn't true?
You look at me now with a glare.
My dream has altered to a nightmare.

Tears are swelling up in me
As I struggle with the fear and anxiety.
Trying to cope with this new reality.
Obscure visions come to me.

What happened to dreams and goals?
Why did you let this madness unfold!!
Was our dream really so unique and rare
That now our dream has become a nightmare.

Wake up now, my brother in deen,
Renew our bond and renew our dreams.
Fight off the perils of shaitan
Ward off this nightmare
And re-establish our bond.

BETTER BROTHERS

Real men
Where are you now?
We need you at home,
Not out in the streets
Constantly on the prowl,
We know your struggles
and your unrelenting pride.
But, is that any reason
to run away and hide?

You hide your strength and sensitivity
You deny your love
And most of all you hide yourself from me.
We sisters have our share of struggles too,
But the difference is
We want to climb up with you.

And all our efforts go in vain,
When you pick up the needle
Or swear my name.
One of the greatest horrors I've yet to see,
Is when you, my brother
Take your rage out on me.
How many women must suffer this way?
Used and abused
for the problems in the world today.

So don't allow things to get so rough.
You must be strong!
You better get tough!
Stop putting the sisters down.
Our existence is a blessing, fortunate to be around
Rise up!! All men of color

And return to being the Better Brother.
And return to being the Better Brother!

I Love You Only If I Am King

Your loves not based on you and me
Cause you don't love me unconditionally.
Your love is based on
Do I meet all your needs,
only if you're happy, only if you're pleased.

So you love me now
You love me today
But by tonight,
If things don't go your way
You'll turn on me
Like a knife to a brother,
You'll even talk about finding another.

You love me not for Allah's pleasure.
You dose it out, you have to measure.
How much have you served today?
And just how much you can take away.
Once those three little words are said,
Communication is over, now straight to bed.

Do whatever you're told to do
Go along with anything I say too.
You can lie, deceive, and get your till,
And expect me to jump when you say at will.
You love me now; you love me today,
But what happens when I don't do as you say?

I remember when you were loving,
But now you're straight out bugging!
Your loves not based on you and me
Cause you don't love me unconditionally.
Loving me when it's good for you,
Hating me as if we're through.

I was starting to buy into the fantasy
That here is someone especially for me,
Who will treat me with kindness and respect
A tender love, but never neglect.
But I'm observing through rose colored shades
My vision tinted by a lovers haze.

You only love me if you are King
But every great King needs a great Queen.
So love me when I'm right,
Love me when I'm wrong
And if we're fortunate,
Our love will remain strong.
As King and Queen.
We can be happy as long as we're both pleased.

SAY IT NOW

Say what you have to say
Please say what you have to say
Before it's too late
Before you can no longer be heard
Before distance obscures your words
Say what you have to say
Before all this goes away
Do what you need to do
Forget past wrongs
To thy own self be true
Just close your eyes
And open your heart
Then say what you have to say
Before past wrongs become the presence of a new day
Turn to all the people who bring you joy
Let them know they are a blessing to you
Love them abundantly and freely too
Tell your spouse and family
Let your sons and daughters know
That they are truly loved
Precious adornments of this world
So release your love before you go.

PART THREE

Loves Stories

LOVE OF COURSE

Love
Can find you
And blind you
Come from behind you
Obsessively bind you
And still you want more

Love
Can rock you
And shake you to the core
It can sneak up behind you
And leave you
Yearning for more

Love
Can linger
And make you believe
Love can stay
And love can leave

Love
Can leave residuals of pain
Make you feel you're going insane
It can break you
And forsake you
And leave you
With remorse

Love
Can hurt you
Desert you
   Yet
You still want more
   Of course.

INNER AWAKENING OF JOY AND BLISS

Timeless........
Ageless
Is how I feel
when we're together
everything has more appeal
Without exception
I appreciate so much more
long dormant senses
take adventure
to explore
Savory meals
arouse my palate
while an assortment of smells
are sensual and aromatic
Attentively I hear only beautiful sounds
from all of Gods creatures
Earth bound
In your presence
I'm more alive and vibrant
You are a joy to me and a God sent
You have taught me my loveliness
In words
In caresses
M y passion awakened
In long endearing kisses
I am thankful
and appreciate
everything so much more
This inner bliss I've come to adore.

MY BELOVED

There is no bond deeper
Than love, united in true faith
There is no bond more fulfilling
Than this mercy and this grace
I believe that love can last a lifetime
And I want to spend that lifetime
Loving you
I love you way down deep to my soul
With you, everyday happiness unfolds
I love the passionate embraces
And the lingering good-byes
In all the sweet, unspoken possibilities
Each time I look into your eyes
You make me smile
And help me grow
I'm more fulfilled and complete
Even more than I can show
Deep within my heart of hearts
Where there are no words
No sounds
What once was lost
Is no longer
For now I've finally found
An endearing love
Who wants to stick around
You have filled an empty space
By your laughter
And your warmth
Your tenderness and strength
Leaves me yearning for even more
Before you, the space was always empty
Waiting just for you
And now I'm filled in the beauty

Of our love
And the harmony we share too
My soul mate, my partner
I wish to spend the rest of my life with you

My beloved husband

TONIGHT..........

Thank you for the wonderful contrast
you bring to my life.
my companion, my love, my friend
you are my passport to paradise
On you, I see reflection
of myself
Warm and kind
generous and loving
Your beauty
creates a splendid melody
in my heart
which I treasure
During the times
we are apart
your voice echoes
In my mind
I'm not isolated
even now from you
Your strong presence
is with me, even when I'm alone
my lonely heart is waiting for you at home
Images of your smile and laughter
bring me much joy
visual memories for me to explore
from sunset to sunrise
I find happiness
when I look in your eyes
in discovering new ways to please
and comfort you
I longingly await
your arrival
For dinner for two.
tonight……..
you, me and the allure of candle light.

NIGHT VISION

In the stillness of the night
Precious stars shining bright.
The silhouette of the moon
Shines with a luminous glow
Under night time skies
Nearby rivers flow.
The sensation of the breeze
As it bends and sways the trees
And soothes the mind and tingles up my spine
Tonight,
I closed my eyes
To star-lit skies.
Anticipating the gracious serene of slumber.
Instead, I see your face
And the beauty of your smile.
Grandly alluring and alive.
A picturesque presence,
A vision of manliness
Shadows of dreams and wants
Dancing in unison,
Across the dark screen of imagery
Loosing my self to heartfelt memories.
Coaxing me from the depths of repose,
Awakening my body and stirring my soul.
My thoughts are aroused as I look into your eyes
Travel your face and observe your smile.
Simple things can last a great while.
So subtly the night creeps away,
Expressing the dawning of a new day.
But that night vision remains on your face
No sign of weariness, not even a trace.

YOU CAN.........

You can come back
When you want to
Just know that I'll be there.
I have yet to climb
To the second floor
I haven't even left the stairs.

You can come back
When you want to
Though you have
Journeyed far
Just know that I'll be here,
For you're still
Lingering In my heart

You can come back
To long ago rooms
Where carpets not on the floor
Where stillness sits
Amidst
The barren walls
I 'm reaching landings
Made it to the second floor

You can come back
If you want to
Before I finally
Shut the entrance to the door.

Imagine there's No Tomorrow

Where does my heart beat now?
Where is the echoes through the night?
Where is the dawn before daylight?
Once we were one mind
Aligned in one time,
Now we walk our different ways,
distant and remote in a murky haze.
If we could only see like we did before.
Before the thunder, before the roar!
Imagine there's no tomorrow
No time for regrets, remorse, or sorrow.
Imagine I couldn't see your face, it would all
Mean nothing if I didn't have the chance to say.
If I didn't say something before it all goes away.
For sure I know each day is a gift,
A touch, a smile, a tender kiss,
Ample blessings to treasure,
That will infinitely be missed.
There are no accidents, nor mistakes
So wherever you are
I will love you always for Allah sake.
For it is all in the creator's hand
Even if I have yet to understand…

WHEN WE'RE APART

When you're away
I stand apart
And whisper
To your image
In my heart
And my thoughts
       Travel
One by one
Across the Earth
Beneath the sun
Until they reach
Awaking ears
Thoughts of love
For you only to hear
When you're away
I stand apart
And whisper
Your sweet name
This will hold me for a while
Until illusions become clear
And I see you face again.

SIDESTEP

We started our dance
    In unison
     Two step
Was all we knew
Married young couple
    In love
One plus one equals two

With many unexpected road blocks
      We parted
   And traveled our separate ways
How did we end up with different partners
Our love we gave, betrayed

SIDESTEP

A detour along our destination
Left us traveling on another road
Now we're traveling solo
Not knowing what will unfold
       Unattached
Single lonely travelers
On an unpredictable winding road.
A spark of light
Illuminates the night
Rescuing our once held romance
And delivers our twining souls
Reminiscent of a second chance.

I'M HERE

I know what you've been through
And baby I'm here for you
I'll do whatever I need to
 Remove what he did to you
I'm here to
 renew you
 relieve you
 restore you
 reward you
 reassure you
remind you
that I'm here love
and I'm here for you
rely on me
and you will see
I won't stop
Until I recapture your joy
and give you the love you deserve.

AN INVITATION

Come walk in my heart
There are soft meadows
To lay and part
Come recline and unwind
Our bodies intertwined
Relax to the gentle breeze
As only you can please

Dream your dreams softly
Cast fear far away
Roll laughing and playing
In blossoms and daffodils
A bed of fresh roses
Is ours to till

Underneath the skies blue
Our canopy suspended
Just for two
The Earth is a spacious place to rest
Until mornings dawning
Or the moons crest
Let's enjoy this fantasy
Come walk in my heart
There are many meadows to see.

Run Away With Me

Why not
Let your heart
Run away with me
To destinations unknown
Limitless possibilities
In unfamiliar zones
Definite locations
To visit and perceive
Far-reaching past
The externals
And hidden facades
An abundance of
Romance
On this long
Anticipated ride

LET YOUR HEART RUN AWAY WITH ME

To expeditions unknown
A trip to ecstasy
As this spacious Earth
We roam
Like an eagle
Spread wings
Soaring high
And free
We can reach our
Destination
If you would

         Let your heart run away with me.

PART FOUR

The Precious Earth

OUR PRECIOUS EARTH

We must tell our children
That the ground beneath their feet
is the ashes of our ancestors
to be protected and preserved to keep
They must respect the land
Abundant in fertile soil
with the lives of their kin
who worked hard and toiled
An abiding place of all things that lived and grew
The rich soil that is soothing, cleansing and healing too
Whatever fate befalls the Earth
ultimately befalls man
We are all custodians
Of our broad and spacious lands
Resilient, firm, and steadfast
composed of mountains and hills
 and plateaus of grass
Mysterious and beautiful
like the magnificently done
Pyramids and Grand Canyon
All things are kindred
Filled with essence beneath the sun
Away from nature a man's heart
can become hard
Lacking respect for living things
Will leave his mind and heart marred
Our changing Earth
Over time, the continents shift
Leaving less land remaining
While our waters continue to drift
What will become of our great bountiful lands?
If we don't preserve it, all may perish under sinking sand.

THE AIR WE BREATH

AIR
Light and breezy
Tingling and pleasing
Soft winds that blow
During all seasons
In winter the winds blow strong
Moving things around
Sometimes causing harm
With a mighty force
It can make your car switch lanes
With the impact of a imperiling hurricane
Air can even fan a fire
Making it roar faster and higher
It can topple buildings
And knock over trees
It can knock out power
With one strong breeze
It can cool you off
Or help you sleep
Cause turbulence in water
And make odors reek
Bad air can kill plants and make you ill
 Ruin rivers and oceans
Lay heavy and still
But, clean fresh air
Feels good and invigorates the mind
Removing old cob webs and problems behind
Until it picks up speed once more
Leaving nothing in place
It can all be destroyed.

"FIRE"

Fire nourishes
But, it can also destroy
It must be respected
Not treated as a toy
It's hot, explosive
Blazing and intense
It's dangerous and deadly
Burns swiftly without pretense
It can be uncontrollable
Hard to contain
Sweeping through swiftly
Until nothing remains
Wipe out forest and all the trees
Everything in the wilderness
That exist so free
It can destroy homes
And take a life
Swiftly churning
In a blink of an eye
It can scorch and burn
Yet provide light
On a dark and starless night
 It can be calming
As you watch it dance
Flickering in the air
Provokes romance
As a candle lit
It provides light on a dark and moonless night
By the fireplace we watch and sit
It can even seer through steel
But yet something about fire
Has such great appeal.

Our Vast Waters

WATER
A powerful force
It can put out a blazing fire
And flood and wash away the Earth
It can carve through a rock
Or create a new path
It can be narrow as a stream
Or a raging river moving fast
It can destroy iron
Or be a source of energy
Generating power
Occurring naturally
It can be grand as an ocean
Outstretched and vast
Extending beyond sunset's overcast
All living things need water to survive
Without water, no living creature would remain alive
It is soothing, cleansing, and purifying,
Thirst quenching and reviving
Rivers, oceans, lakes, and streams
They can be quiet and still
Engaging thoughts and will
Or mighty with turbulence and rift
No matter how you see it
Water is a precious gift.

RAINDROPS

Sunny skies
are turning gray
the wind is blowing
every which way
Rain is falling
lightly at first
and then skies open
a rambunctious burst
Drenching rain can wash away the Earth.
puddles of water on the ground
flooded neighborhoods in every town
The roar of thunder is abound.
lightning afflicts a striking blow
carving through any thing as it goes
In the sky, the clouds transform to red
and on the earth the ground is fed.
purified and nurtured
as the sun shines bright
shadows of color appear through the light
Clouds disappear once more
as the rain ends
land is dry
upon a rainbowed beautiful sky.

Autumn Stirring

The leaves of the trees are changing
To vibrant colors with each passing day
Graduating from shades of natural greens
To hues of golden brown
While sunny skies disappear to gray
As the winds of Autumn have scattered the leaves
To create a kaleidoscope burial shroud

Returning those of ripened age
Once blossoming flowers
Back to the Earth from whence they came
A gradual change is creeping upon us as we sleep
Autumn's presence is stirring right beneath our feet
To hasten the arrival of the fallen leaves
The impatient wind gives them a thrust
Mixed with bouquets of dead flowers
Colors of bright orange, red, and rust

Forming a natural blanket on the ground
As we walk along its shield
The sound of the leaves
Rustling around
On the streets and in the fields
Tells us
Autumn is here

The crackling of the leaves
Reminiscent of summers's cooling
The gentle breezes
Always feels good
For now it's Autumn that's blooming
Autumn is stirring
Seasons are changing
This is my favorite time
Whenever it is occurring.

MORNING WALK

The sun shines bright
A sparrow takes flight
Tree limbs swinging
Birds singing
Branches of trees
Swaying in the breeze
Flowers are at their peak of colors
A kaleidoscope of
Pinks, purple, and shades of green.
Lawn hoses spraying
Water twirling all around
While squirrels are playing
In the grass on the ground.
Butterflies dancing in the air
The joy of summer is everywhere.
Bees buzzing
Lawn mowers humming,
The streets are void of much traffic
In the early hours of morning
A good view of the sun rise
A clear day, blue skies.
Limitless possibilities
Unknown opportunities
Another day to make the scale of good deeds high
And remember and worship our Lord.
To rise above mediocrity
And strive to be the best we can be.
Every day blessings are abound,
You'll will find them if you just look around.
A quiet walk through the neighborhood
Can be beneficial and yield much good.

SEVEN DAYS

Melancholy Mondays
Always make me blue
Cause on Monday mornings
There's always too much to do
Staff meetings after a grueling work day
I keep asking myself
There's got to be a better way

Tailor made Tuesdays
Is when things begin to fit
When everything runs smoother
And task get completed it
Because Tuesdays are always pretty terrific

Wonderful Wednesdays
Is a turning point in the week
Some people refer to it as getting over the hump
But I see it as rising out of a slump
Business is handled
Errands are run
Looking at the big picture
Knowing I got everything done

Tranquil Thursdays
Is a really good day
You are tireless
And grateful
Blue skies
No longer gray
The week-end is approaching so near
Happiness dwells washing away
All doubts and fears
Fabulous Fridays
Is the best day of the week

When you can hear a great khutbah
And afterwards get something good to eat
Joy and contentment is innate
Work files are done organized and neat
You feel good
That you made it through another week
Saturday is upon us
Now you can catch up on your sleep

Sensational Saturdays
You do your errands and chores
Get a take out lunch
To enjoy eating outdoors
Sometimes you just ride up
On bargains galore
Frequent garage sales
Or markets and stores
Saturdays are never a bore

Superb Sundays
Is a day to relax
Reflect on the week
And just kick back
Evaluate the days past
And figure out how next week
Can be better than your last
Seven days of the week come to an end
Tomorrow another week begins
And once again
Melancholy Monday descends.

Winter's Solace

Gradually winter comes
Creeping in
No thunder and lightning
No great world winds
And as the winds begin to blow
Softly at first
Then it changes to snow
Suddenly the world
Stands still
Everything freezes
Strong winds promote harsh breezes

A mantle of white
Snow flurries
Plummeting down
A frosty winter scene
Burying deep
Everything in its path
Is covered with sleet

A formidable snow drift
And a winters chill
The streets are abandoned
And everything stands still
The serenity of a winters day
Means no going to work
But kids can go outside to play

A winter wonderland
Creates a moment of solace
For all Gods creatures
Including man

THE GIFT OF A TREE

A thing of beauty for all to see
The blessing of one single tree
The largest plant upon the Earth
Gives us countless blessings
Immeasurable worth
It gives us fruits and nuts to eat
Some are sour and some are sweet
And upon your branches, stretched out high
Countless rows of chirping birds stop by
To perch upon your branches long
And sing all morning their beautiful song
From the bountiful leaves that grow
Children design crowns for their heads
And beneath the tree, a story is read
Behind a tree is fun to play hide and seek
Until weary, under the shade he sleeps
Young children love to climb and play
And when they become older
They utilize the wood
For a warm place to stay
Or to build a magnificent boat
To take them far away
When there's nothing left of the tree to give
But one lonely stump perched on a hill
It stills provides a place to sit and rest
Until another tree gives her all, her best.

It's a Spring Thing

Spring signifies
The arrival of color
Fragrances of lilies and daffodils
What a dazzling display
Of luscious flowers
Everything is alive and vibrant
People moving about are so excited
All things are fresh and new
After the cocoon of winter
We all want a new hairdo
Everyone is tired of hibernating inside
It just feels good
To take a long ride
It's like the world wakes up
From a three month slumber
To ride their motorcycles and over-sized hummers
Welcoming the sunny skies
And the blossoming of flowers
 Anticipating a mid-day thunder shower
It's a spring thing
Love is in the air
Romances blossom
And marriages begin everywhere.

AFRICA

You are Africa to me
Each breath you take
It's clear to see
You're homesick
For the motherland
The clear blue ocean
 Submerged in desert sand

You are Africa to me
A vision as lovely as a tree
Whose roots are embedded strong
Broad shoulders
And long arms
Richness and robust
Mandingo warrior
Mighty and vigorous

Like a smoldering ember
A man on fire
Your voice bellowing higher
And higher
Tight and booming
Like the sound
Of the duff
Raw and sensuous
Sometimes a little rough
A resonant boom

Africa looms
You are my home
My Islamic country
Is where I belong
This is what I need to see
Where Islam
Is the primary focus

Not like some in western society
Half-witted
Yet, thinking they're free

You are Africa to me
Delve into its mystery
A long hidden history
 Waiting covertly for you
My migrant king
My heart feels this too.

EGYPT

We witnessed the great temples and majestic mosques
with all their legacy and beauty
These magnificent structures rose out of the barren desert
Towering the Earth
serene and full of wonder
as if somehow a miraculous rebirth
Engulfed by sand and sea over centuries ago
Where Pharaohs once ruled
Neferritti, Hatshebat, and Cleopatra too.
These were all black women who once ruled
In ancient Egypt, while Europe was cast in the dark ages
Egypt was progressing gradually, advancing in stages.
excelling in mathematics, literature, and science too
a melting pot of knowledge for those who knew.
Where remains of Pharaohs lay dormant
only impressive monuments left behind
deciphered hieroglyphs
tapestry rich and divine
treasure laden tombs
a sanctuary for those who ruled.
Amid the rumbled mountains
Shifting colors of sky and sand
An emotional pilgrimage
to this promised land.
Where here is a rich endowment of faith
Extra-ordinary beauty and magnificent landscapes
Exuberant market places with bargains galore
It Is Here you'll find a sale for sure
On camel back we rode through this non-worldly terrain
A safari in the kings valley
From desert region then back to the city again
In the morning we sailed on the Nile
Reflecting and contemplating for a while
This is where our home should be
In this incredible fertile land by the sea.

Mesmerizing secrets-overwhelming me
Brilliant colors of sky and shadows of sand
Towering pyramids in this vibrant land.
A clear and mystifying night
The stars and the moon illuminated bright
The Mediterranean our view to see
It was here we found our place
And I rediscovered me
A journey, a rite of passage
Of self-discovery
We also learned a lesson in Black history.

PART FIVE

Ties That Bond

FRIENDSHIP

A friend
Is like a beautiful stone
It takes many years to cultivate
Many years to grow
Stones do not change within themselves
They change through outside forces
A friend can influence you to grow
And often relationships change courses
Take care that disagreements
Don't destroy in an instant
That which took a life time to build
For when a stone is broken
It takes a long time to congeal.

LOVING MOTHER

Among the richest blessing
That this life could ever bring
Is a kind and thoughtful mother
Whose love means everything
You've given so much love
Yet, asked so little in return
You've taught me so many lessons
Even what I thought I'd never learn
Throughout the years
Your caring has always been there
I'm happy for the treasured memories that we share
You have taught me what true love really means
And that some people who come into your life
Aren't really what they seem
Your comfort and inspiration
Are blessings that I adore
You will forever remain in my heart
From this day and forever more
Mom I love you
And I thank-you
For all you've done for me
I will always be grateful
And love you eternally.

TO MY SON, WITH LOVE

Son,
When I look into your eyes
I still see the reflections of
The little boy you were
In the man you are now
I've love you son
With my whole heart and soul
From the first time I saw you
And counted your fingers and your toes
I like knowing that some things never change
Your smile
Your sensitivity
Your laughter
And my love for you always remains
I hope you always know
That I'm thinking of you
No matter near or far
Or wherever your journey takes you to
I forever want
Your complete happiness in life
A life filled with joy
Where dreams and goals are fulfilled
And all the answers to your questions
 Are readily revealed
I wish you the resilience
To bounce back from suffering
And begin again
With your head held high
There's no limit
To your potential
When you let your light shine
We have walked many paths
On our way from yesterday
But, as I look back
I wouldn't want it any other way

You are the most precious gift
A parent could receive
Know that I'll always love you
And that you can trust and believe.

Phone Call

Sometimes I feel the need
for human exchange
I want to expand
share my joy
and dabble in my pain
An opportunity
to touch another soul
talk about our plans and goals
Sharing thoughts,visions,and dreams
day to day trials
and what it all means.
Sharing moments
brings such pleasure
In a world gone wrong
nothing can measure
A friend can remind you
just be strong
and be patient
with whatever is going on.
Your phone call came
right on time
put me in a better
frame of mind
So when you feel the need
To dialogue
just pick up the phone
and give me a call.

CHILDREN SPEAK

Our children
Are trying to tell us something
And we're not listening
They speak of crime and drugs
Gangs roaming close to our doors
They speak of peace
Violence, the killings, and war

They say to the elders
Won't you please listen?
In our world
Something is missing

Fathers in the household
Are a rare commodity
From the suburbs
To the urban inner cities
Children are being raised
With only one role model
Mothers are playing a dual role
While the children are growing up quicker
And getting more out of control.

Responsibility doesn't end at conception
Many kids never even seen a father in action
Fathers need to be responsible
For their families
Because this leads to a break down
In our communities
How can we teach our daughters
How to choose a good man
When all they see
Is Moms weary hands
How can we teach our sons
The role of a man

When they can't understand
Why their fathers abandoned
Away from the family
Absentee dads
It's hard to conceive
How can they break the cycle
When they are grown
If unavailable fathers is all they've known

It takes two responsible adults
To raise our children
A balance of love, nurturing
Discipline and approval
Fathers must participate
In their children's lives
So that they can
Make good decisions
And be productive and wise

We can't let our children
Be raised by the streets
We must help them
Before they're in too deep
Lured by peer pressure
To do all sorts of things
Encouraged to lose their modesty
Ignore their own minds
And just follow the lead
We must show them how
To acknowledge their own voice
And prevent them from making
Bad decisions, poor choices
No obstacle
Cannot be overcome
A challenge for many
An opportunity for some

Our children
Are trying to tell us something
Sometimes not in words
But
In their actions they speak
Beckoning to be heard
Listen elders
Pay attention
To what they say
For if they can't speak it
They will behave
In a self-destructive way

We can no longer
Be unconscious
To our youths problems
We must become a village
And work together
To abolish them

Our children
Are trying to tell us
Something in their lives
Is missing!

Are we listening?

SISTER LOVE

I always have something
To be happy about
Because I will always
Have you for a sister
And that counts without a doubt
A great blessing
To have you as a good friend
You mean so much to me
We share such wonderful memories
The time shared with you
Through happiness and sorrow
Lends a hope for many tomorrows
Thank-you
For always being there
Looking out for me
And showing that you care
We have seen our children grow
From boys to men
And now we enjoy our grandchildren
With all the blessings they send
My dear sister
Know that I love you
And I hope we'll always be friends
For without your kindness and love
Life as I know it would surely end.

INTUITION

That little voice
That silent speaks
Soft to perceive at times
Without a silent retreat
This is when I crave solitude
To hear that voice
That tells me what to do.
Right away it changes my mood
Guidance comes
Clarity rules
Questions answered
In solitude.

CONTENT

A day so beautiful
Yet I chose to stay indoors
tidy up the house
and
mop and wax the floors
Too beautiful
a day
to stay inside
but
I had chores to do

So curtains parted
I observed
as the sunlight
radiated through

Washing up the dishes

Finally
Throwing out
The sprouting potatoes
The wilted lettuce
and shrunken tomatoes
I suddenly discover
a feeling of content
From
staying inside
and
Choosing how
this beautiful day
I spent.

Marriage Dua

Oh Allah
The magnificent
Bless and sustain
This union
Place love and mercy
In our hearts
Keep us guided
   By Quran and Sunnah
And never ever depart
Keep negative thoughts
And fitnah away
Bless this happy household
   Each and every day.

Fill our home with love
And an atmosphere of tranquility
May I respect all of his rights,
And he respect those of me.
May we both put our best forward
And cherish this magnificent gift
   By doing what's right
   Avoiding what's wrong
And never intentionally doing harm.
   Give us patience and compassion,
         Understanding
         Never too demanding
A most valuable union that must be
         Treasured
   A commitment that cannot
         Measured
      To Allah (Most High)
      Do we only worship.

PART SIX

Reflections

Nobody can make it all Alone

Sitting here contemplating
How I'm going to make it on my own
Finally resigned from work
All my children are grown
Grandchildren are growing up so fast
 Frequent visits to grandma's house
Will become a thing of the past
As they embrace having kids of their own
These four walls
Mark a corner stone
Where jilted memories
Are free to roam

Economy is at an all time low
Even millionaires are running scared
From fear of losing everything they had
But wealth doesn't come with joy
You have more possessions
To work harder for
And no matter how many, you still want more
As I ponder now
Just how I feel
One thing is clear, one thing is real
No one makes it through this life's ordeal
By doing it all alone
Nobody but, nobody
Can survive in this world alone
Sometimes you need a nurturing hand
Someone who equally understands
That being alone is not the way to go
Because Nobody but, nobody
Wants to do it all alone.

Attachments

Some people are lost without going to work
If they lose their job
Panic-stricken and berserk
There job replaces all that's missing in their life
Tireless toiling can't make them feel right
A continuum of a daily rat race
Until this isn't enough, so they quicken the pace
Some people stay in a constant pursuit of wealth
Even to the detriment of their well-being and health
A frantic and frenetic pace
An attempt to deny what they're terrified to face
Others live through their children's lives
By keeping them so busy
Day and night
Striving to have them reach their old dreams
Until the kids are all grown
Then life is not what it seems
Now for them it's clear to see
It's not in their children where they should put their belief
Some people live for their pets
Treating them like children
Instead of dogs and cats
Dressing them in fine clothing
With coats and hats
Kissing and patting them
Even allowing them in bed
As if this is their spouse
To whom they wed
But this world is full of amusement and play
Caught up in this worldly life they slave
Caught in illusion
From the cradle to grave
Robbing them of great blessings
For it's really contentment they crave.

DREAMS

Instill in me dreams
Big and small
Short term
Long term
I want them all
Grandeur dreams
To visualize
And hold

Instill in me dreams
So I may fly
Past unwarranted fears
Soaring high
Inspire me
To use my talents and skills
To be a service to others
And do Gods will

Dream by dream
Until these tiny ideas
Grow to greater aspirations
Then what now seems clear
And all my goals
Are manifesting before my eyes
I'm grateful and joyous
But I'm not surprised!

READ, READ, READ

Do you want to go to China, Japan,
Africa or the Philippines?
Do you want to explore vast lands
And have big dreams?
Then pick up a book, open up, and read
You'll be surprised at what you may see
Travel to Egypt or the Mediterranean Sea
You can journey anywhere in the world
You desire to be.
A good book
Opens up the world to you
Expands your horizons
and your vocabulary too.
It lets you see beyond
Your four corners
And limitless possibilities
All this can happen when you delve in and read
You can travel to exotic places
Swim in the deepest oceans
Or climb the largest glaciers
Even orbit to unknown spaces
Reading enriches your life in so many ways
It's better than sitting in front of the t.v. all day
Nourish your mind
Spend some quality time
With a good book today!!!!!!

A Mind Is a Terrible Thing To Waste

Johnny can't read
Johnny can't write
Johnny thinks hanging in the streets is tight.
All through life
Johnny skips school.
He uses any excuse,
because he thinks that's cool.
He gets high all day
on pills and smoke.
Until this isn't enough,
so then he tries dope.
Hooked on a habit, He wish he could rid.
And now Johnny feels sorry
for what he did.
But, Johnny can't read
And Johnny can't write.
Now, Johnny gives up hope
He has lost all insight.
Devoid of the warmth of family and friends
To make this burden seem less
All Johnny can see is despair
And his self-destructive mess.
No job, no education, and no real friends,
He thinks to himself, "If I could only live my life again!"
 Alone and bitter, living life in a tailspin
Frustrated and alienated, He wonders when will this end?
"Stop the world," he cries!" I want to get off!"
Then don't bother me
Cause I can't cope.

Just leave me alone,
or get me some more dope.
Hooked on a habit,
Its name is Crack.
And there's no doubt,
Once you try it;
It's hard to turn back.

Well, Johnny tries living once again
He walks the hot pavement all day.
As he talks to himself, while looking for work,
"There has got to be a better way."
I can work he cries
Just give me a try!
Oh no! They gave the job to
The educated guy.

Oh Johnny, if you had only stayed in school
Cause as you can see
doing drugs, isn't cool.
But Johnny can't read
And Johnny can't write.
So now, he's lost all reason and foresight.
Johnny overdosed today.
A wasted mind ,
Lays buried in the grave.
He could have been a doctor, a writer, an artist,
A teacher, a lawyer, a scientist,
Or even an engineer,
But instead Jonny lies dead.
His life is over at the tender age of 23.

A Dark Path

Fear has become his closet friend
It's taken over
His body and soul
It's relentless
He's losing all control
Just like the past
He can't let it go
Anger has begun
To rule each day
Replacing joy and happiness
With anger and despair

Unsavory characters
Violence, drugs and madness
Have left their dismal mark
Secrets are lurking
 And they are deep and dark
Mistrust and suspicion
Run through his veins
Piercing his heart
With animosity and pain
Manipulation and lies
Have become his game

His demeanor has changed
Heart is turning to stone
Self-destruction is winning
Down to the bone

Doesn't he know
Fighters always lose
Pain pervades the path
He willingly chooses
I'll hurt them first

Before they hurt me
Even if injured
Unintentionally
The dark path
He travels alone
Mind is dissolving
As he continues to roam
Running away
From so much pain
Bloodshot eyes
Shows he's going insane

Lay down your pain
Let go of the past
What's the purpose
In this constant rehashing
Repeating the same things
Over and over again
Results don't change
And you can never win

DREAM IN COLOR

If you're going to dream
Dream in color
Let your dreams be vivid
Full of freshness and newness
Lifelike images
Brilliant and distinct
Royal deep colors
Passionate and unique

If you're going to dream
Dream on a grand scale
Your dreams can become your reality
If you're not afraid to fail
Picture a place you want to go
The earth is spacious
As you well know
Dream of things that may seem beyond your reach
Set your intention
And then pursue what you seek
Ask for what you want in your life
Don't procrastinate
No need to think twice
If you're going to dream
Dream out loud
Speak as though it already exist
No dream worth having
Is far out of your midst
Visualize it as already received
See it, believe it, expect
That it's on its way
Everything comes in divine timing
Just be patient until that day!

SET ME FREE

I was almost convinced
Love could win this time
And being this happy
Took a long time to find
It seemed possible to live
Without regrets and remorse
For love is such a powerful force
But, your love for me
   I will never know
Your heart said stay
But, instead you chose to go
   So how can you say
You want to be with me
When you were the one who set me free?
After the loss of releasing me
    You now expect to see
 me fly back into the cage
clipped winged and dazed
from deception and lies
  Myriads of hellos and good-byes
        I don't perceive
 being stung from the same hole twice
this new perch shall suffice
on the back of the winds
til the current ends
 I will remain free
  From being deceived
  Over and over again.

ONCE AGAIN MAYBE

Maybe, I'll always wonder why
Maybe I would feel better if I could cry.
Maybe we will live and learn
Maybe we will just crash and burn.
Maybe now he's come to stay.
Maybe he will go away.
Maybe he will slip again
Or maybe our marriage will win.
Maybe he will make it right
Maybe he will just drop out of sight.
Maybe I will leave with regret
Maybe we'll wish we never met.
Maybe this can make us grow
Maybe I'll never know.
Maybe all this is meant to be
Maybe in time we too shall see.
Meanwhile, maybe I'll get hurt.
Should I run? Should I desert?
Maybe your love will shine
Maybe, it's just another line.
Perhaps we've sunken to an all time low.
Should I pack my bags, say goodbye, then go?
Just maybe, this time it will work
If you get yourself together, stop being a jerk.
Maybe all this confusion will go away
If I could make up my mind to leave or to stay.
Maybe this is just another test
Mom always told me you will know what's best.
Maybe if we take it real slow
Over time that's when I'll know.
Maybe we will get through it all
We just might wind up having a ball.
You know I'm not sure what to do
So maybe I should just ask you.
Well, maybe????

BURIED DEEP

Unhealed emotional wounds
From childhood
Or a woman scorned
Residuals of pain
When a relationship
Goes wrong
Ancient grudges
Brooding inside
Expecting the past
To mirror the rest of her life

So we build invincible fences
Around our hearts
With signs that read
Don't go beyond this point
Don't enter! please
I'm terrified of intimacy

Self-constricted walls
That shouldn't exist
Solitary confinement
To remain alone
But
Now I'm loosening
This stranglehold
Slowly letting go
And letting my feelings unfold
Releasing my guard
And watching love explode

Giving love freely
And expecting love in return
After all these experiences
I've finally learned.

LIVING LIFE

Can you remember?
Not so long ago
How we struggled
Just to get by.
Couldn't seem to get ahead
No matter how hard I tried.
At the end of the week
The paycheck was small,
Barely enough, barely nothing at all.
I had to rob Peter, just to pay Paul.

Couldn't buy you the latest sneakers and shoes
Designer clothes you had but a few.
Tried to keep you focused in school.
While every day, I felt fatigue and abused.
Weary from work, but chores to do.
I helped you with school work while I cooked,
Fixed you dinner, then sometimes read you a book.

Times were tough; Days were long
A single parent on her own.
Had to keep a roof over our head,
Food on the table, belly fed.
Paycheck wasn't making a dent,
But at least it did pay the rent.
I use to tell you to hold on,
You got to survive, you must stay strong.
Trouble doesn't come to stay for long.
If you can just make it through this night,
Things will look better in the morning light.
After struggling for such a long time,
Finally it's time for me to get mine.
For the years of struggle and sacrifice
It's time I got paid
For this life of strife.

So now, I'm grateful I can enjoy the day.
Ultimately, now I can do things my way.
Never have to use lay-away again
Cause now I got the cash to spend.
Bought me a house in the suburbs,
And a Lexus car was a nice splurge.

A new chapter in life is beginning
And the old way of life
Is coming to an ending.
I'm overjoyed that life has given
Me a little time and grace
After 30 years in the workman's place.

I can retire now
While I'm still in good health
Sit back, relax, plan vacations
And spend my wealth.
Living Life

Grown Woman

In the sunset of her life
   She decided
No more tears
No more strife
And to love herself
   Unconditionally
She gathered up
 All her injured dignity

Even though 55
Was drawing near
And she was in the
Sunset of her years
She had such a youthful grace
   And just in case
She hadn't made it clear
Not another day
Would she shed sad tears

Fine lines illustrated
    Her face
Determined to defy
Her bodies haste
The young girl
Vanishing without a trace

No more issues
To resolve or erase.
She's at a level of maturity
Feeling even better
Than in her late twenties
For after all
She's learned to
Maneuver in this world
With confidence

As a woman
Not like a young girl
A work in progress
Concluded most efficiently
Done with grace
So eloquently
Thoughts moving faster
      Than I can
         But
        Finally
She's a grown woman.

About the Author

Nailah Abdus-Salaam was born in Kinston, North Carolina. Her formative years were spent in the urban city of East Orange, New Jersey where she later returned after graduating from Hampton University in Virginia. She returned back to her early roots to serve as a Junior High School teacher where she worked for over thirty years, desiring to make a difference in her community. Her focus has always been on education and motivating others to strive to reach their full potential.

She is also an entrepreneur with her own small business and a freelance writer. She has had samples of her work published in Essence magazine and Azizah magazine, a magazine for the contemporary MuslimWoman, and an Anthology of poetry entitled Beneath the Winter sky.

She has been under the inspiration of writing poetry since her youth, and finally to see the realization of her first book of poetry to be published is a dream come true.

When she isn't writing, she enjoys studying Arabic, Islamic Studies, horse back riding, and working with the youth.

Printed in the United States
149439LV00005B/1/P